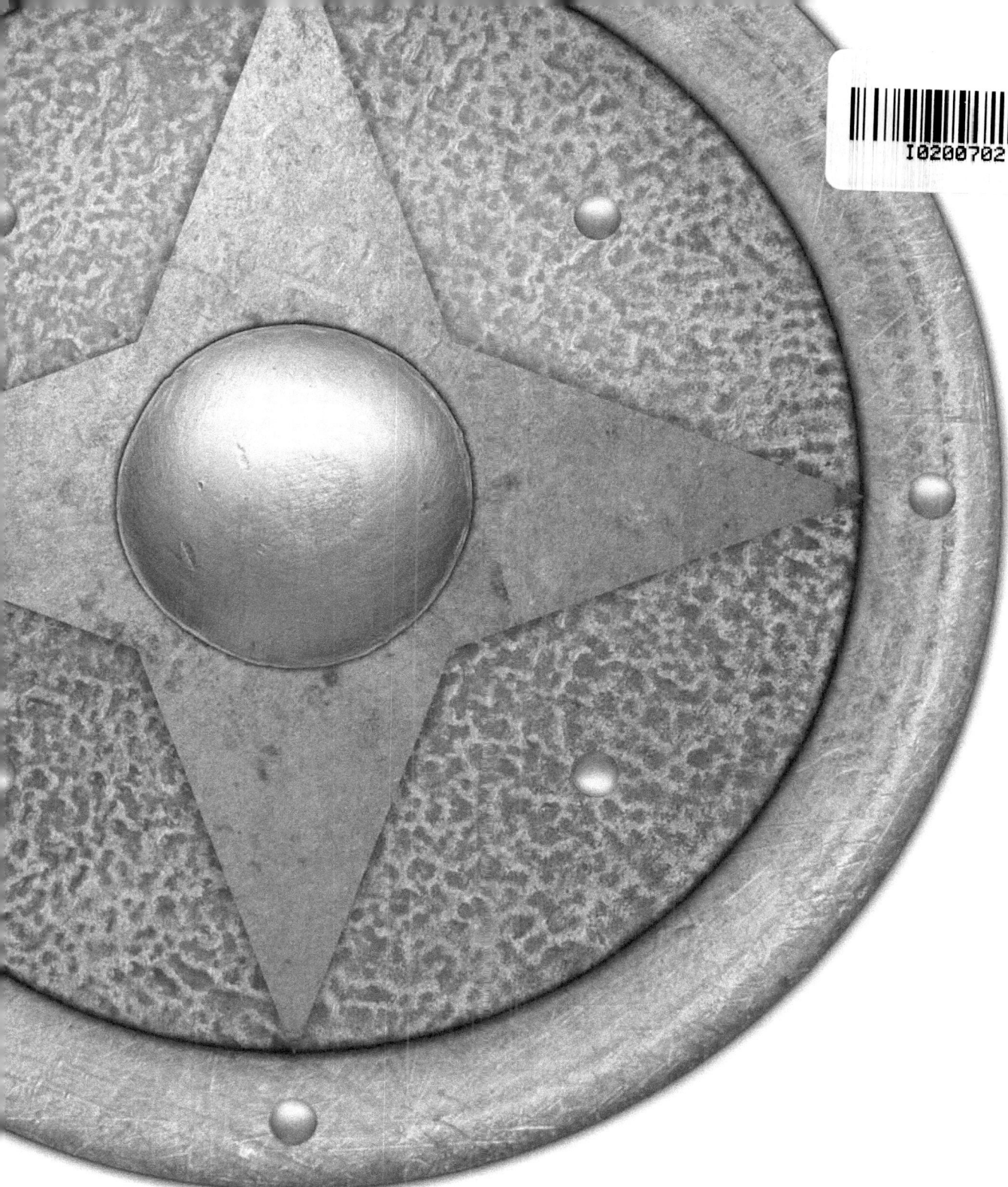

Unshakeable Kingdom
Unwavering Warrior

Rev. Dr. Don L. Davis

SIAFU
MEN'S CONFERENCE
2015

The Urban Ministry Institute,
a ministry of World Impact, Inc.

We dedicate this booklet to those

Dedicated Spirit Warriors of Christ

those who endure hardness
in order to fulfill their call with honor,
who follow God's biblical wisdom strategy,
who sacrifice time, talent, and service for the Kingdom,
and who patiently endure trial and suffering on behalf of Christ
in order that his Kingdom might be advanced and his name glorified
among the most vulnerable people in the cities of the world.

May God grant them his Spirit and his strength
as they fight for the unshakeable Kingdom
as unwavering warriors
in service to the risen King,
Christ Jesus.

See that you do not refuse him who is speaking. For if they did not escape when they refused him who warned them on earth, much less will we escape if we reject him who warns from heaven. [26] At that time his voice shook the earth, but now he has promised, "Yet once more I will shake not only the earth but also the heavens." [27] This phrase, "Yet once more," indicates the removal of things that are shaken – that is, things that have been made – in order that the things that cannot be shaken may remain. [28] Therefore let us be grateful for receiving a kingdom that cannot be shaken, and thus let us offer to God acceptable worship, with reverence and awe, [29] for our God is a consuming fire.

~ Hebrews 12.25-29

Table of Contents

"Take the sword!"

~ Lord Bartok's order to Commander Raiden in the graveyard, passing to Raiden his sword, and bestowing on him the privilege and responsibility of protecting the Bartok kingdom and name.

"The wounds of honor are self-inflicted."

~ Lord Bartok on the meaning of honor, reflected both in his refusal to be bribed by the emperor's lackey, and the unbreakable code of honor taken by his own knights of the realm.

"Tonight our enemy will bear witness of the unbreakable code of the 7th rank. We will reclaim what they tried to take, we will restore the name of our master, the voice of our people, and the spirit of our nation."

~ Commander Raiden's speech to the disavowed knights of the Bartok clan before they engaged the council of Geeza Mott.

**"Your fathers honor has been reclaimed.
The Bartok name will never be forgotten."**

~ Commander Raiden's word of assurance to Lord Bartok's daughter after their successful raid on Mott's fortress.

"Unshakeable Kingdom, Unwavering Warrior"

Our theme for the 2015 SIAFU Men's Conference is *Unshakeable Kingdom, Unwavering Warrior*. It is built on the biblical theme of urban disciples of Jesus serving as unwavering warriors for the advance of God's unshakeable Kingdom. We are following the storyline of the film *Last Knights*, a moving story of a fallen warrior who rises up to overthrow a corrupt, sadistic ruler in order to avenge his dishonored master, and to restore his master's heirs to their rightful place of authority and honor. With honor, courage, and perseverance, these knights planned and carried out an operation over time that would liberate their master's heirs, eliminate the shame brought to his house, and restore the honor associated with his name.

"We have planned, sacrificed, and waited
for the right moment – and now – it is time."

~ Commander Raiden to his fellow knights on the eve of their
dramatic strike against the corrupt leaders of the empire

Last Knights

As unwavering warriors of Christ,
let us embrace the unbreakable code of honor,
take the sword given to us by our Master,
and let us fight for the Kingdom
to the honor of Jesus Christ.

Unshakeable Kingdom, Unwavering Warrior

Living as a Warrior of Honor

Session 1

Work the Plan

Learn the Discipline of Following Strategy

SIAFU 2015 Men's Conference

Dr. Don L. Davis

Unshakeable Kingdom, Unwavering Warrior
Don L. Davis © 2015. All Rights Reserved.

Chorus

Unshakeable kingdom, unwavering warrior
Of the Lord Almighty (yeah, yeah, yeah, yeah!)
Unshakeable kingdom, unwavering warrior
Of the risen King (unshakeable, unshakeable) (repeat)

Verse

It won't be shaken, this blessed Kingdom we've received
Can't be mistaken', it'll run for all eternity
We fight for honor, with hearts of gratitude and fear
Consuming fire, our holy God has now appeared

Verse

We've heard the call, we're moving out
We're ready for the fight,
We've got a plan, we'll sacrifice
And when it's right – we'll strike!
And when the victory is won
We'll glorify our King
And with the voice of triumph shout
To him who set us free

Share in Suffering as Good Soldiers of Christ Jesus

You then, my child, be strong in the grace that is in Christ Jesus; and what you have heard from me through many witnesses entrust to faithful people who will be able to teach others as well. Share in suffering like a good soldier of Christ Jesus. No one serving in the army gets entangled in everyday affairs; the soldier's aim is to please the enlisting officer.

~ 2 Timothy 2.1-4 (NRSV)

Work the Plan:
Learn the Discipline of Following Strategy

The Warrior's Code

As brothers called by God, we confess Jesus of Nazareth as Lord, God's only Son and our Master and King. We represent his Kingdom, and seek to please him in our relationships and conduct. We will follow his plan, sacrifice everything for his glory, and learn to wait on his timing and direction alone. Our one life aim will be to glorify Jesus wherever we go, in whatever we say or do, no matter what we face or have to endure. We will strive to be men of honor, Christ's band of brothers, living as unwavering warriors for the unshakeable Kingdom of God Amen!

~ An Affirmation of Our Victory in Christ

SESSION 1

Work the Plan
Learn the Discipline of Following Strategy

Rev. Dr. Don L. Davis

Soldiers of Christ Win by Working God's Plan

Soldiers win the victory by learning how to use the Lord's weapons faithfully, skillfully, day by day, repetition after repetition. God has a plan to train us, to use us, to make us effective, but it requires faithful practice, done in the midst of situations where our struggles and challenges are vexing us. We win the day by working the plan, not in miraculous rescues and dramatic shifts. One step at a time, one hill at a time, one battle at a time – that is how we become victorious.

- **Start small, don't quit:** expect difficulty, misery, and tribulation, and be prepared to go through, not around, Gal. 6.7-9.
- **Bear all things:** don't allow excuses to hide a lack of discipline, 1 Cor. 13.7; 2 Tim. 3.12; Acts 14.22.
- **Don't be ashamed to suffer:** resistance of the enemy involves struggle which is the key to achievement, 2 Tim. 1.8; James 4.7; 1 Pet. 5.8-9.
- **Endure all for the sake of God's people:** the more you learn to suffer, the better you learn to serve, 2 Tim. 2.10.
- **Take courage from Jesus' example:** he endured much for the sake of triumph that awaited him, Heb. 12.1-3; John 16.33; 15.20-21.

As unwavering warriors of the Kingdom, we must fight together to liberate our generation from the domination of the devil.

As unwavering warriors of Christ's unshakeable Kingdom, we must learn to . . .

- WORK THE PLAN: *Learn the discipline of following strategy*
- *Make the Sacrifice:* Unconditionally surrender all to represent Christ
- *Learn to Wait:* Endure trial and struggle as you seek God's leading and will

I. Contact: Is there a plan for the universe, and us?

_____

The Universe Is at War – Choose a Side

According to the Bible, our lives are lived in the midst of an invisible spiritual war. One of the most dangerous things we can do is simply to ignore this reality. We accept the Bible as true but we often live as though the battle existed on some far-off mission field, not here in our city. The fact is, there is a battle raging over your city and it is affecting you right now. . . . Every one of us faces demonic forces in our local environment, but as Christians we are called to a bigger battle. We are contending for our whole generation. We are called to act locally but to think globally.

~ John Dawson. *Taking Our Cities for God*, pp. 27, 29.

_____

what's
the
plan?

What is the biblical plan for turning all things around and setting things right?

Who is in charge of the universe? Are things always going to have to be like this? Is God in charge? If he is, what is his plan to work everything out okay?

Spend some time thinking about what you know or have heard about God's plan for the world, and list it out below, step by step, in the lines provided. What do you believe God's plan for the universe is?

1. _____

2. _____

3. _____

4. _____

5. _____

6. _____

7. _____

8. _____

9. _____

10. _____

II. Content: We're Invited to Participate in God's Plan to Redeem Creation through His Son.

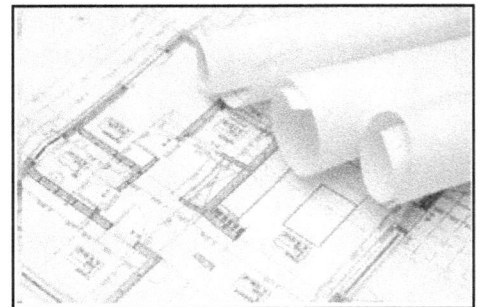

A. DEFINE THIS TIGHT.
God's plan, from the very beginning, has been to crush evil and rebellion in his universe. The universe is at war!

1. *This is a battle for supremacy: Who ultimately should be recognized as the final ruler of all things?*

a. Exod. 15.11 – Who is like you, O LORD, among the gods? Who is like you, majestic in holiness, awesome in glorious deeds, doing wonders?

b. Deut. 5.7 – You shall have no other gods before me.

c. Deut. 6.5 – You shall love the LORD your God with all your heart and with all your soul and with all your might.

2. *This is a battle for authority: Whose will should prevail in all matters of creation and destiny?*

See Appendix 1,
*The Story of God:
Our Sacred Roots*

  a. Isa. 43.10 – "You are my witnesses," declares the LORD, "and my servant whom I have chosen, that you may know and believe me and understand that I am he. Before me no god was formed, nor shall there be any after me."

  b. Isa. 44.8 – Fear not, nor be afraid; have I not told you from of old and declared it? And you are my witnesses! Is there a God besides me? There is no Rock; I know not any.

3. *This is a battle for glory: Who is worthy to receive the praise and glory for the splendor of creation and life?* Ps. 115.1-3 – Not to us, O LORD, not to us, but to your name give glory, for the sake of your steadfast love and your faithfulness! [2] Why should the nations say, "Where is their God?" [3] Our God is in the heavens; he does all that he pleases.

The Fight Is On!
God declares that, because of sin and rebellion, the entire universe is at war. Since the creation of the universe, a battle has been raging in the heavenlies where God has determined to rescue the universe from the effects of the curse of Satan and the first human pair. Everything is at stake, and not one square inch is not being contested. It is a knock-down, drag-out warfare for the final control and destiny of creation. It is a battle for preeminence in the universe!

From Before to Beyond Time:
The Plan of God and Human History
Adapted from Suzanne de Dietrich, God's Unfolding Purpose. Philadelphia: Westminster Press, 1976.

I. Before Time (Eternity Past) 1 Cor. 2.7
   A. The Eternal Triune God
   B. God's Eternal Purpose
   C. The Mystery of Iniquity
   D. The Principalities and Powers

II. Beginning of Time (Creation and Fall) Gen. 1.1
   A. Creative Word
   B. Humanity
   C. Fall
   D. Reign of Death and First Signs of Grace

III. Unfolding of Time (God's Plan Revealed through Israel) Gal. 3.8
   A. Promise (Patriarchs)
   B. Exodus and Covenant at Sinai
   C. Promised Land
   D. The City, the Temple, and the Throne (Prophet, Priest, and King)
   E. Exile
   F. Remnant

IV. Fullness of Time (Incarnation of the Messiah) Gal. 4.4-5
   A. The King Comes to His Kingdom
   B. The Present Reality of His Reign
   C. The Secret of the Kingdom, the Already and the Not Yet
   D. The Crucified King
   E. The Risen Lord

V. The Last Times (The Descent of the Holy Spirit) Acts 2.16-18
   A. Between the Times: the Church as Foretaste of the Kingdom
   B. The Church as Agent of the Kingdom
   C. The Conflict between the Kingdoms of Darkness and Light

VI. The Fulfillment of Time (The Second Coming) Matt. 13.40-43
   A. The Return of Christ
   B. Judgment
   C. The Consummation of His Kingdom

VII. Beyond Time (Eternity Future) 1 Cor. 15.24-28
   A. Kingdom Handed Over to God the Father
   B. God as All in All

See Appendix 2, *From Before to Beyond Time: The Plan of God and Human History*

B. BREAK IT DOWN! God's plan was to send a Savior who would crush the rebellion of the devil, fulfill his covenant promise to save his creation, and save all people who believe in his Champion, Jesus Christ the Lord.

1. *It's an ancient plan.* Gen. 3.15 – I will put enmity between you and the woman, and between your offspring and her offspring; he shall bruise your head, and you shall bruise his heel.

2. *It's an adopted plan.* Eph. 2.1-7 – And you were dead in the trespasses and sins [2] in which you once walked, following the course of this world, following the prince of the power of the air, the spirit that is now at work in the sons of disobedience – [3] among whom we all once lived in the passions of our flesh, carrying out the desires of the body and the mind, and were by nature children of wrath, like the rest of mankind. [4] But God, being rich in mercy, because of the great love with which he loved us, [5] even when we were dead in our trespasses, made us alive together with Christ – by grace you have been saved – [6] and raised us up with him and seated us with him in the heavenly places in Christ Jesus, [7] so that in the coming ages he might show the immeasurable riches of his grace in kindness toward us in Christ Jesus.

3. *It's an announced plan.*

   a. Matt. 28.18-20 – And Jesus came and said to them, "All authority in heaven and on earth has been given to me. [19] Go therefore and make disciples of all nations, baptizing them in the name of the Father and of the Son and of the Holy Spirit, [20] teaching them to observe all that I have commanded you. And behold, I am with you always, to the end of the age."

b. Mark 16.15-16 – And he said to them, "Go into all the world and proclaim the gospel to the whole creation. [16] Whoever believes and is baptized will be saved, but whoever does not believe will be condemned."

c. John 20.30-31 – Now Jesus did many other signs in the presence of the disciples, which are not written in this book; [31] but these are written so that you may believe that Jesus is the Christ, the Son of God, and that by believing you may have life in his name.

C. CHECK THIS OUT. God's plan is to call and equip warriors who are deputized to make disciples among the nations.

See Appendix 3,
*Jesus of Nazareth:
The Presence
of the Future*

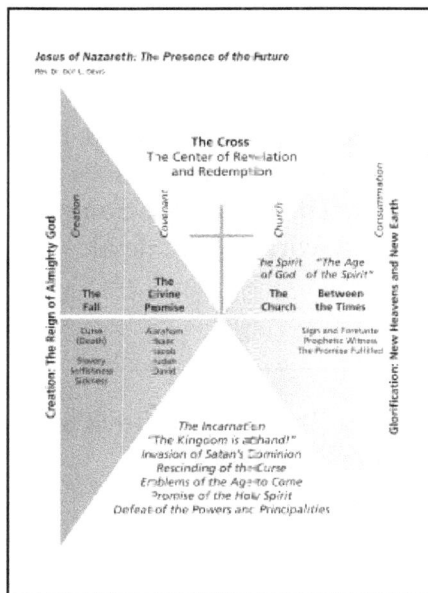

Jesus of Nazareth: The Presence of the Future

1. *Everything is at stake.* Rom. 8.18-21 – For I consider that the sufferings of this present time are not worth comparing with the glory that is to be revealed to us. [19] For the creation waits with eager longing for the revealing of the sons of God. [20] For the creation was subjected to futility, not willingly, but because of him who subjected it, in hope [21] that the creation itself will be set free from its bondage to corruption and obtain the freedom of the glory of the children of God.

2. *Everyone is involved.* John 3.16-17 – For God so loved the world, that he gave his only Son, that whoever believes in him should not perish but have eternal life. [17] For God did not send his Son into the world to condemn the world, but in order that the world might be saved through him.

3. *Every evil will be put down.*

   a. Rev. 1.17-18 – When I saw him, I fell at his feet as though dead. But he laid his right hand on me, saying, "Fear not, I am the first and the last, [18] and the living one. I died, and behold I am alive forevermore, and I have the keys of Death and Hades."

   b. Col. 2.15 – He disarmed the rulers and authorities and put them to open shame, by triumphing over them in him.

   c. 1 John 4.4 – Little children, you are from God and have overcome them, for he who is in you is greater than he who is in the world.

   d. 1 John 3.8 – Whoever makes a practice of sinning is of the devil, for the devil has been sinning from the beginning. The reason the Son of God appeared was to destroy the works of the devil.

God's Plan: Jesus Was Sent to Destroy the Devil's Work, the Instigator of the Universe's Rebellion

Knowing their thoughts, he said to them, "Every kingdom divided against itself is laid waste, and no city or house divided against itself will stand. [26] And if Satan casts out Satan, he is divided against himself. How then will his kingdom stand? [27] And if I cast out demons by Beelzebul, by whom do your sons cast them out? Therefore they will be your judges. [28] But if it is by the Spirit of God that I cast out demons, then the kingdom of God has come upon you. [29] Or how can someone enter a strong man's house and plunder his goods, unless he first binds the strong man? Then indeed he may plunder his house. [30] Whoever is not with me is against me, and whoever does not gather with me scatters."

~ Matthew 12.25-30

III. Connection: We Must Commit Ourselves to Work the Plan God Revealed in Christ.

    A. THE KEY PRINCIPLE. *Work the plan that the Lord has established.* Ps. 33.11 – The counsel of the LORD stands forever, the plans of his heart to all generations.

    B. THE LORD'S PLAN CANNOT BE FRUSTRATED.

        1. *No one can upset God's plans.*

            a. Job 23.13 – But he is unchangeable, and who can turn him back? What he desires, that he does.

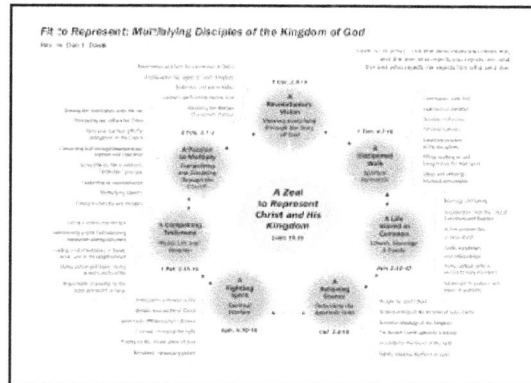

See Appendix 4, *Fit to Represent: Multiplying Disciples of the Kingdom of God*

            b. Prov. 19.21 – Many are the plans in the mind of a man, but it is the purpose of the LORD that will stand.

            c. Isa. 14.24 – The LORD of hosts has sworn: "As I have planned, so shall it be, and as I have purposed, so shall it stand."

        2. *His plans are always deeper than you think.*

            a. Ps. 92.5 – How great are your works, O LORD! Your thoughts are very deep!

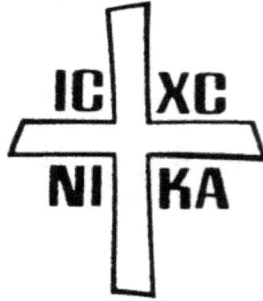

b. Isa. 55.8-9 – For my thoughts are not your thoughts, neither are your ways my ways, declares the LORD. [9] For as the heavens are higher than the earth, so are my ways higher than your ways and my thoughts than your thoughts.

3. *God's plan is to give us a future and a hope.* Jer. 29.11-13 – For I know the plans I have for you, declares the LORD, plans for welfare and not for evil, to give you a future and a hope. [12] Then you will call upon me and come and pray to me, and I will hear you. [13] You will seek me and find me, when you seek me with all your heart.

God's warriors follow God's plans!

To be a warrior of Christ is to make a clear, bold commitment to follow his plan – to do his will, follow his orders, and to never shrink back. You can identify those who belong to Christ by those who act on his will, who obey his commands and follow his plans, no matter what.

They please their commanding officer. 2 Tim. 2.3-4 – Share in suffering as a good soldier of Christ Jesus. [4] No soldier gets entangled in civilian pursuits, since his aim is to please the one who enlisted him.

They keep the Captain's commandments. John 15.10-14 – If you keep my commandments, you will abide in my love, just as I have kept my Father's commandments and abide in his love. [11] These things I have spoken to you, that my joy may be in you, and that your joy may be full. [12] This is my commandment, that you love one another as I have loved you. [13] Greater love has no one than this, that someone lay down his life for his friends. [14] You are my friends if you do what I command you.

They follow his plan through thick and thin. John 14.21-24 – "Whoever has my commandments and keeps them, he it is who loves me. And he who loves me will be loved by my Father, and I will love him and manifest myself to him." [22] Judas (not Iscariot) said to him, "LORD, how is it that you will manifest yourself to us, and not to the world?" [23] Jesus answered him, "If anyone loves me, he will keep my word, and my Father will love him, and we will come to him and make our home with him. [24] Whoever does not love me does not keep my words. And the word that you hear is not mine but the Father's who sent me."

The Kingdom shall be established . . .
And in the days of those kings the God of heaven will set up a kingdom that shall never be destroyed, nor shall the kingdom be left to another people. It shall break in pieces all these kingdoms and bring them to an end, and it shall stand forever.

~ Daniel 2.44

God's Plan Is for You to Join the Fight!
Every Christian is a walking battlefield. Every believer carries deep within himself a terrible conflict. And most of us will gravitate to anything that will help us win the battle. Call it the battle between the flesh and the spirit. Call it the quest for the victorious Christian life. Call it what you want. But it's a flat-out-knock-down- drag-out war. And when it's over, you want to be among those who are still standing. The principles of war are taught in military academies all over the world. In most ways, spiritual warfare is no different than physical warfare. Every soldier who expects to not only survive but win must understand and employ these principles in his own daily battles "against the powers of this dark world and against the spiritual forces of evil in the heavenly realms" (Ephesians 6.12b NIV).

~ Stu Webber. *Spirit Warriors*.
Sisters, OR: Multnomah Publishers, 2001, p. 16.

As unwavering warriors of Christ's unshakeable Kingdom, we must learn to . . .

- WORK THE PLAN: *Learn the discipline of following strategy*
- *Make the Sacrifice:* Unconditionally surrender all to represent Christ
- *Learn to Wait:* Endure trial and struggle as you seek God's leading and will

Unshakeable Kingdom, Unwavering Warrior

Living as a Warrior of Honor

Session 2

Make the Sacrifice

Unconditionally Surrender All to Represent Christ and His Kingdom

SIAFU 2015 Men's Conference

Dr. Don L. Davis

Unshakeable Kingdom, Unwavering Warrior
Don L. Davis © 2015. All Rights Reserved.

Chorus

Unshakeable kingdom, unwavering warrior
Of the Lord Almighty (yeah, yeah, yeah, yeah!)
Unshakeable kingdom, unwavering warrior
Of the risen King (unshakeable, unshakeable) (repeat)

Verse

It won't be shaken, this blessed Kingdom we've received
Can't be mistaken', it'll run for all eternity
We fight for honor, with hearts of gratitude and fear
Consuming fire, our holy God has now appeared

Verse

We've heard the call, we're moving out
We're ready for the fight,
We've got a plan, we'll sacrifice
And when it's right – we'll strike!
And when the victory is won
We'll glorify our King
And with the voice of triumph shout
To him who set us free

Share in Suffering as Good Soldiers of Christ Jesus

You then, my child, be strong in the grace that is in Christ Jesus; and what you have heard from me through many witnesses entrust to faithful people who will be able to teach others as well. Share in suffering like a good soldier of Christ Jesus. No one serving in the army gets entangled in everyday affairs; the soldier's aim is to please the enlisting officer.

~ 2 Timothy 2.1-4 (NRSV)

Make the Sacrifice:

Unconditionally Surrender All to Represent Christ and His Kingdom

The Warrior's Code

As brothers called by God, we confess Jesus of Nazareth as Lord, God's only Son and our Master and King. We represent his Kingdom, and seek to please him in our relationships and conduct. We will follow his plan, sacrifice everything for his glory, and learn to wait on his timing and direction alone. Our one life aim will be to glorify Jesus wherever we go, in whatever we say or do, no matter what we face or have to endure. We will strive to be men of honor, Christ's band of brothers, living as unwavering warriors for the unshakeable Kingdom of God. Amen!

~ An Affirmation of Our Victory in Christ

SESSION 2

Make the Sacrifice
Unconditionally Surrender All to Represent Christ and His Kingdom

Rev. Dr. Don L. Davis

The Enemy Hinders Our Life of Sacrifice through Emotional Reactions

Our problem is that we have become so accustomed to believing our feelings as though they were facts. *We never examine them. We never take them and look at them and ask, "Is this true?"* We simply say, "I feel this way. Therefore it must be true." This is why so many are constantly defeated; they accept their feelings as facts. Rather, we are to say, "Christ is my righteousness. I am linked with him. I am one with him. His life is my life and my life is his life. We are married. Therefore, I cannot believe this lie that these evil thoughts are my thoughts. They are not my thoughts at all. They are thoughts which come because of another force. It is not my thinking at all. No, it is the Devil again. I do not want these thoughts. I do not like them. I reject them. I do not want them in my thinking; therefore they are not mine. They are the Devil's children, and I'll spank them and send them back where they belong!"

~ Ray Stedman. *Spiritual Warfare.*
Waco, TX: Word Books, 1976, p. 129.

As unwavering warriors of the Kingdom, we must fight together to liberate our generation from the domination of the devil.

SESSION 2: MAKE THE SACRIFICE • 33

As unwavering warriors of Christ's unshakeable Kingdom, we must learn to . . .

- *Work the Plan:* Learn the discipline of following strategy
- MAKE THE SACRIFICE: *Unconditionally surrender all to represent Christ*
- *Learn to Wait:* Endure trial and struggle as you seek God's leading and will

I. Contact: What Is the Meaning of True Sacrifice for Christ?

Realizing Christ's Authority

The center of dispute in the whole universe relates to who has the authority. We have to contend with Satan by asserting that authority is with God. We have to set ourselves to submit to God's authority and to uphold God's authority. We must meet God's authority face-to-face and have a basic realization of it. Before Paul realized authority, he wanted to eradicate the church from the earth. But after he met the Lord on the way to Damascus, he realized that it was difficult to kick against the goads (God's authority) with his feet (man's energy). He immediately fell down, acknowledged Jesus as Lord, and submitted to the instruction of Ananias in Damascus. Paul met God's authority. At his conversion, Paul was brought not only into *a realization of God's salvation,* but also into *a realization of God's authority* [italics mine].

~ Watchman Nee. *Spiritual Authority.* p. 3

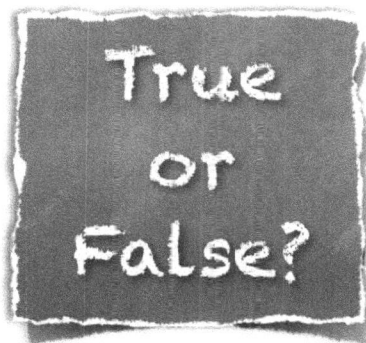
True or False?

Answer the following statements on the nature of sacrifice as either true or false.

Spend some time thinking about what you know or have heard about sacrificing and surrendering all for Christ, to fulfill his plan for the world. Circle the correct answer, as you understand it.

T or F   1. It is possible to serve Christ our captain with honor without sacrifice.

T or F   2. Everyone who lives godly in Christ will certainly be persecuted for it.

T or F   3. Jesus' statement, "A servant is not greater than his master," means that we should expect to be honored in the same way that Jesus was honored, whether we endure what he did or not.

T or F   4. Only some of Christ's soldiers are called to suffer and sacrifice for his name's sake.

T or F   5. Extreme devotion to Christ demands that we stand our ground, no matter what, till the end.

T or F   6. To be a living sacrifice involves only being willing to give all to Christ, not actually doing it.

T or F   7. The plan that God has may or may not include great sacrifice for us and our loved ones.

II. Content: We're Called to Sacrifice Our Lives for Christ to Fulfill His Call on Our Lives.

A. DEFINE THIS TIGHT. In order to execute God's plan as one of his warriors, you must be ready to sacrifice all for his honor and glory.

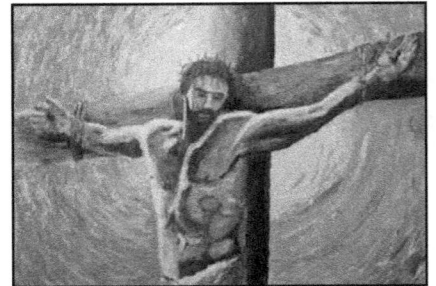

1. *We died with Christ to sin.*

    a. John 12.24-26 – Truly, truly, I say to you, unless a grain of wheat falls into the earth and dies, it remains alone; but if it dies, it bears much fruit. [25] Whoever loves his life loses it, and whoever hates his life in this world will keep it for eternal life. [26] If anyone serves me, he must follow me; and where I am, there will my servant be also. If anyone serves me, the Father will honor him.

    b. Rom. 6.3-5 – Do you not know that all of us who have been baptized into Christ Jesus were baptized into his death? [4] We were buried therefore with him by baptism into death, in order that, just as Christ was raised from the dead by the glory of the Father, we too might walk in newness of life. [5] For if we have been united with him in a death like his, we shall certainly be united with him in a resurrection like his.

2. *We died with Christ to the world.*

    a. Matt. 10.38-39 – And whoever does not take his cross and follow me is not worthy of me. [39] Whoever finds his life will lose it, and whoever loses his life for my sake will find it.

    b. Gal. 6.14 – But far be it from me to boast except in the cross of our Lord Jesus Christ, by which the world has been crucified to me, and I to the world.

    c. 2 Tim. 2.3-4 – Share in suffering as a good soldier of Christ Jesus. [4] No soldier gets entangled in civilian pursuits, since his aim is to please the one who enlisted him.

3. *We died with Christ to the flesh (our "self," i.e., old sin nature).*

    a. Gal. 2.20 – I have been crucified with Christ. It is no longer I who live, but Christ who lives in me. And the life I now live in the flesh I live by faith in the Son of God, who loved me and gave himself for me.

    b. 1 Tim. 1.18-19 – This charge I entrust to you, Timothy, my child, in accordance with the prophecies previously made about you, that by them you may wage the good warfare, [19] holding faith and a good conscience. By rejecting this, some have made shipwreck of their faith.

Christ's Sacrifice Is the Fuel of the Missionary Movement

White-hot faith is the fuel that missionary movements run on. Nothing happens without a deep dependence on God. Nothing leads us into a healthy dependence on the power of God more than to come face to face with our desperate need of him. Jesus is the Apostle and Pioneer of our faith. He led the way for us in surrender to the will of God and the power of the Holy Spirit.

~ Steve Addison

B. Break it down! We cannot follow God's plan without making the sacrifice that the plan requires. *No sacrifice, no plan!*

1. *It's a hard sacrifice.* 2 Cor. 4.7-12 – But we have this treasure in jars of clay, to show that the surpassing power belongs to God and not to us. [8] We are afflicted in every way, but not crushed; perplexed, but not driven to despair; [9] persecuted, but not forsaken; struck down, but not destroyed; [10] always carrying in the body the death of Jesus, so that the life of Jesus may also be manifested in our bodies. [11] For we who live are always being given over to death for Jesus' sake, so that the life of Jesus also may be manifested in our mortal flesh. [12] So death is at work in us, but life in you.

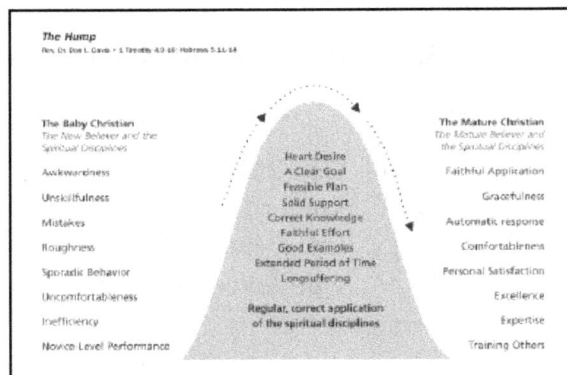

See Appendix 5, *The Hump*

2. *It's a common sacrifice.* 1 Pet. 5.8-10 – Be sober-minded; be watchful. Your adversary the devil prowls around like a roaring lion, seeking someone to devour. [9] Resist him, firm in your faith, knowing that the same kinds of suffering are being experienced by your brotherhood throughout the world. [10] And after you have suffered a little while, the God of all grace, who has called you to his eternal glory in Christ, will himself restore, confirm, strengthen, and establish you.

3. *It's a daily sacrifice.*

See Appendix 6,
Steps to Equipping Others

a. Luke 9.23-26 – And he said to all, "If anyone would come after me, let him deny himself and take up his cross daily and follow me. [24] For whoever would save his life will lose it, but whoever loses his life for my sake will save it. [25] For what does it profit a man if he gains the whole world and loses or forfeits himself? [26] For whoever is ashamed of me and of my words, of him will the Son of Man be ashamed when he comes in his glory and the glory of the Father and of the holy angels."

b. 1 Cor. 15.31 – I protest, brothers, by my pride in you, which I have in Christ Jesus our Lord, I die every day!

c. Rom. 8.35-37 – Who shall separate us from the love of Christ? Shall tribulation, or distress, or persecution, or famine, or nakedness, or danger, or sword? [36] As it is written, "For your sake we are being killed all the day long; we are regarded as sheep to be slaughtered." [37] No, in all these things we are more than conquerors through him who loved us.

Laws of Sowing and Reaping

See Appendix 7, Laws of Sowing and Reaping

C. **Check this out.** We sacrifice to fulfill God's will because Jesus did for us. *As he did, so we must do.*

1. *God forms us as we surrender. Christ's Spirit helps us as we share in his sufferings.*

   a. Isa. 64.8 – But now, O LORD, you are our Father; we are the clay, and you are our potter; we are all the work of your hand.

   b. Rom. 8.14-17 – For all who are led by the Spirit of God are sons of God. [15] For you did not receive the spirit of slavery to fall back into fear, but you have received the Spirit of adoption as sons, by whom we cry, "Abba! Father!" [16] The Spirit himself bears witness with our spirit that we are children of God, [17] and if children, then heirs – heirs of God and fellow heirs with Christ, provided we suffer with him in order that we may also be glorified with him.

2. *His sacrifice is now both a model and an example for us.*

   a. Phil. 2.5-8 – Have this mind among yourselves, which is yours in Christ Jesus, [6] who, though he was in the form of God, did not count equality with God a thing to be grasped, [7] but emptied himself, by taking the form of a servant, being born in the likeness of men. [8] And being

SESSION 2: MAKE THE SACRIFICE • 39

found in human form, he humbled himself by becoming obedient to the point of death, even death on a cross.

b. John 13.13-17 – You call me Teacher and Lord, and you are right, for so I am. [14] If I then, your Lord and Teacher, have washed your feet, you also ought to wash one another's feet. [15] For I have given you an example, that you also should do just as I have done to you. [16] Truly, truly, I say to you, a servant is not greater than his master, nor is a messenger greater than the one who sent him. [17] If you know these things, blessed are you if you do them.

Paul the Apostle: God's Plan to Rescue Others Demands That His Soldiers Make the Total Sacrifice for the Sake of the Kingdom

Acts 26.15-18 – And I said, "Who are you, Lord?" And the Lord said, "I am Jesus whom you are persecuting. [16] But rise and stand upon your feet, for I have appeared to you for this purpose, to appoint you as a servant and witness to the things in which you have seen me and to those in which I will appear to you, [17] delivering you from your people and from the Gentiles – to whom I am sending you [18] to open their eyes, so that they may turn from darkness to light and from the power of Satan to God, that they may receive forgiveness of sins and a place among those who are sanctified by faith in me."

Acts 26.19-21 – Therefore, O King Agrippa, I was not disobedient to the heavenly vision, [20] but declared first to those in Damascus, then in Jerusalem and throughout all the region of Judea, and also to the Gentiles, that they should repent and turn to God, performing deeds in keeping with their repentance. [21] For this reason the Jews seized me in the temple and tried to kill me.

3. *As his soldiers, we are called to follow in his steps,* 1 Pet. 2.21-24 – For to this you have been called, because Christ also suffered for you, leaving you an example, so that you might follow in his steps. [22] He committed no sin, neither was deceit found in his mouth. [23] When he was reviled, he did not revile in return; when he suffered, he did not threaten, but continued entrusting himself to him who judges justly. [24] He himself bore our sins in his body on the tree, that we might die to sin and live to righteousness. By his wounds you have been healed.

III. Connection: God's Plan Only Succeeds If We Unconditionally Surrender All to Christ.

A. The Key Principle. *Make the sacrifice so the Lord can use you to work the plan.* 2 Tim. 2.20-21 – Now in a great house there are not only vessels of gold and silver but also of wood and clay, some for honorable use, some for dishonorable. [21] Therefore, if anyone cleanses himself from what is dishonorable, he will be a vessel for honorable use, set apart as holy, useful to the master of the house, ready for every good work.

B. Making the Sacrifice involves waging a Good warfare (1 Tim. 1.18)

1. *Guard your thoughts, trails, tongue, and time.*

a. Guard your *thoughts.* Phil. 4.8 – Finally, brothers, whatever is true, whatever is honorable, whatever is just, whatever is pure, whatever is lovely, whatever is commendable, if there is any excellence, if there is anything worthy of praise, think about these things.

b. Guard your *trails*.

(1) Prov. 3.5-6 – Trust in the LORD with all your heart, and do not lean on your own understanding. [6] In all your ways acknowledge him, and he will make straight your paths.

(2) Col. 3.17 – And whatever you do, in word or deed, do everything in the name of the Lord Jesus, giving thanks to God the Father through him.

c. Guard your *tongue*. 1 Pet. 3.10-12 – For "Whoever desires to love life and see good days, let him keep his tongue from evil and his lips from speaking deceit; [11] let him turn away from evil and do good; let him seek peace and pursue it. [12] For the eyes of the Lord are on the righteous, and his ears are open to their prayer. But the face of the Lord is against those who do evil."

d. Guard your *time*. Eph. 5.15-18 – Look carefully then how you walk, not as unwise but as wise, [16] making the best use of the time, because the days are evil. [17] Therefore do not be foolish, but understand what the will of the Lord is. [18] And do not get drunk with wine, for that is debauchery, but be filled with the Spirit.

See Appendix 8,
*From Deep Ignorance
to Credible Witness*

From Deep Ignorance to Credible Witness

2. *Discipline your body and keep it under control*, 1 Cor. 9.22-27 – To the weak I became weak, that I might win the weak. I have become all things to all people, that by all means I might save some. [23] I do it all for the sake of the gospel, that I may share with them in its blessings. [24] Do you not know that in a race all the runners run, but only one receives the prize? So run that you may obtain it. [25] Every athlete exercises self-control in all things. They do it to receive a perishable wreath,

but we an imperishable. [26] So I do not run aimlessly; I do not box as one beating the air. [27] But I discipline my body and keep it under control, lest after preaching to others I myself should be disqualified.

3. *Quit acting surprised that living for Christ is difficult.* 1 Pet. 4.12-14 – Beloved, do not be surprised at the fiery trial when it comes upon you to test you, as though something strange were happening to you. [13] But rejoice insofar as you share Christ's sufferings, that you may also rejoice and be glad when his glory is revealed. [14] If you are insulted for the name of Christ, you are blessed, because the Spirit of glory and of God rests upon you.

God's Warriors Understand and Freely Make the Sacrifices for Spiritual Battle!

To be a warrior of Christ is to make a clear, bold commitment to follow his plan – to do his will, follow his orders, and to never shrink back. You can identify those who belong to Christ by those who act on his will, who obey his commands and follow his plans, no matter what.

The Church in the West today presents too easy a target for Satan. We do not believe we are at war. We do not know where the battleground is located, and, in spite of our weapons, they are neither loaded nor aimed at the right target. We are unaware of how vulnerable we are. We are better fitted for a parade than for an amphibious landing.

~ Ed Silvoso

We Live Because He Gave His All for Us

For you know the grace of our Lord Jesus Christ, that though he was rich, yet for your sake he became poor, so that you by his poverty might become rich.

~ 2 Corinthians 8.9

Formed by Command; Disciplined by Sacrifice

Jesus' favorite method of teaching his disciples was through formation. Formation comes not by telling people things they should know, but by commanding them to do specific things. Jesus said to the disciples, "Go to such-and-such city. Don't say hello, don't greet anybody in the way. When you get to a house say, 'The peace of God be on this house.' Heal the sick that are in the house. Eat what they give you. Announce that the kingdom of God is at hand, and don't pass from house to house. And if they don't receive you in the house, go on to the next house." Jesus didn't preach inspirational sermons; those are for disobedient people, to convey to them that it would be nice if they would like to do the thing Jesus commanded. So we preach the inspirational message, and while the organ plays and the choir sings, we try to coax people to make decisions – but a decision to what? Jesus didn't suggest or plead; He gave commands.

~ Juan Carlos Ortiz. *Call to Discipleship.*
Plainfield, NJ: Logos International, 1975, pp. 71-72.

As unwavering warriors of Christ's unshakeable Kingdom, we must learn to . . .

- *Work the Plan:* Learn the discipline of following strategy
- MAKE THE SACRIFICE: *Unconditionally surrender all to represent Christ*
- *Learn to Wait:* Endure trial and struggle as you seek God's leading and will

Unshakeable Kingdom, Unwavering Warrior

Living as a Warrior of Honor

Session 3
Learn to Wait

Endure Trial and Struggle as You Seek God's Leading and Will

SIAFU 2015 Men's Conference

Dr. Don L. Davis

Unshakeable Kingdom, Unwavering Warrior
Don L. Davis © 2015. All Rights Reserved.

Chorus

Unshakeable kingdom, unwavering warrior
Of the Lord Almighty (yeah, yeah, yeah, yeah!)
Unshakeable kingdom, unwavering warrior
Of the risen King (unshakeable, unshakeable) (repeat)

Verse

It won't be shaken, this blessed Kingdom we've received
Can't be mistaken', it'll run for all eternity
We fight for honor, with hearts of gratitude and fear
Consuming fire, our holy God has now appeared

Verse

We've heard the call, we're moving out
We're ready for the fight,
We've got a plan, we'll sacrifice
And when it's right – we'll strike!
And when the victory is won
We'll glorify our King
And with the voice of triumph shout
To him who set us free

Share in Suffering as Good Soldiers of Christ Jesus

You then, my child, be strong in the grace that is in Christ Jesus; and what you have heard from me through many witnesses entrust to faithful people who will be able to teach others as well. Share in suffering like a good soldier of Christ Jesus. No one serving in the army gets entangled in everyday affairs; the soldier's aim is to please the enlisting officer.

~ 2 Timothy 2.1-4 (NRSV)

Learn to Wait:

Endure Trial and Struggle as You Seek God's Leading and Will

The Warrior's Code

As brothers called by God, we confess Jesus of Nazareth as Lord, God's only Son and our Master and King. We represent his Kingdom, and seek to please him in our relationships and conduct. We will follow his plan, sacrifice everything for his glory, and learn to wait on his timing and direction alone. Our one life aim will be to glorify Jesus wherever we go, in whatever we say or do, no matter what we face or have to endure. We will strive to be men of honor, Christ's band of brothers, living as unwavering warriors for the unshakeable Kingdom of God. Amen!

~ An Affirmation of Our Victory in Christ

SESSION 3

Learn to Wait
Endure Trial and Struggle as You Seek God's Leading and Will

Rev. Dr. Don L. Davis

The Devil Will Seek to Crush Us by Deception and Wiles
There is much about Satan in the letters of Paul but there is little of direct attack of satanic forces. . . . By far, the majority of attacks of the Devil against Christians are not direct but indirect. That is why they are called the "wiles" of the Devil. Wiliness means deviousness, circuity, something not obvious. We need to examine this more thoroughly, for the major attack of the Devil, and his powers against human life is not by direct means, but indirect – by satanic suggestions through the natural and commonplace events of life.

~ Neil T. Anderson and Dave Park. *The Bondage Breaker*.
Eugene, OR: Harvest House Publishers, 1993, p. 46.

As unwavering warriors of the Kingdom, we must fight together to liberate our generation from the domination of the devil.

As unwavering warriors of Christ's unshakeable Kingdom, we must learn to . . .

- *Work the Plan:* Learn the discipline of following strategy
- *Make the Sacrifice:* Unconditionally surrender all to represent Christ
- LEARN TO WAIT: *Endure trial and struggle as you seek God's leading and will*

I. Contact: Why Is It Absolutely Critical for a Spiritual Soldier to Never Give Up?

Persevering Obedience Is a Soldier's Truest Virtue

Unquestionably obedience is a high virtue, a soldier quality. To obey belongs, preeminently, to the soldier. It is his first and last lesson, and he must learn how to practice it all the time, without question, uncomplainingly. Obedience, moreover, is faith in action, and is the outflow as it is the very test of love. "He that hath My commandments and keepeth them, he it is that loveth Me."

> – E. M. Bounds. *The Necessity of Prayer (elec. ed.).*
> WordSearch Bible Software, 2006.

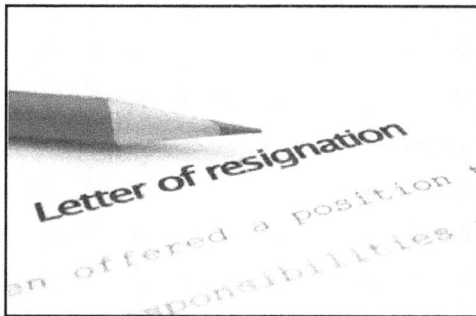

Match the following statements to their corresponding Scripture references.

Test your knowledge of the Scripture's teaching on the nature of persistence, steadfastness, and never giving up.

1. No temptation has overtaken you that isn't common	a. Luke 11.4
2. Lead us not into temptation	b. James 5.11
3. We don't wrestle against flesh and blood	c. 1 Pet. 5.8
4. Job remained steadfast, and so should we	d. 1 Cor. 10.13
5. The devil prowls around looking for someone to devour	e. 2 Thess. 3.3
6. The Lord is faithful, and he will guard and keep us	f. Gal. 6.10
7. We will reap a harvest if we do not give up	g. Eph. 6.12

Reflect on your understanding of learning to wait on the Lord . . .

T or F   1. The temptation to quit is the same as actually giving up.

T or F   2. Every believer must perseverance during trial; no one gets a free pass.

T or F   3. Discouragement is one of the devil's strongest weapons against spiritual warriors.

II. **Content: Every Soldier Must Learn to Be Patient and to Persevere – to Never Shrink Back or Give Up.**

A. DEFINE THIS TIGHT. Perseverance comes out of and because of suffering – we persevere when we endure and overcome trial and trouble.

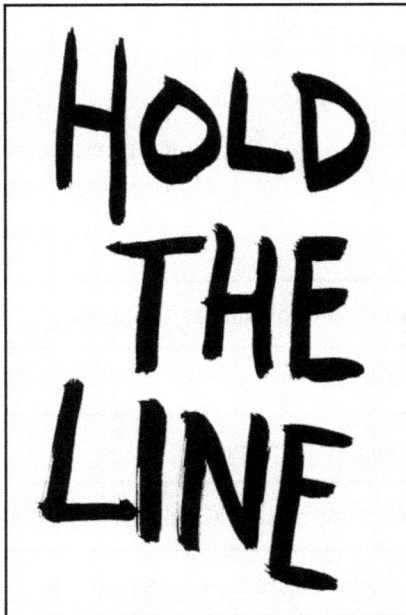

1. *Trouble will come in different sizes, of various kinds, at random times,* James 1.2-3 – Count it all joy, my brothers, when you meet trials of various kinds, [3] for you know that the testing of your faith produces steadfastness.

2. *Perseverance holds up under trials without giving in,* 2 Thess. 1.4 – Therefore we ourselves boast about you in the churches of God for your steadfastness and faith in all your persecutions and in the afflictions that you are enduring.

3. *We must endure hardship, knowing that the Lord will stand by us so we don't quit,* 2 Tim. 3.10-12 – You, however, have followed my teaching, my conduct, my aim in life, my faith, my patience, my love, my steadfastness, [11] my persecutions and sufferings that happened to me at Antioch, at Iconium, and at Lystra – which persecutions I endured; yet from them

all the Lord rescued me. [12] Indeed, all who desire to live a godly life in Christ Jesus will be persecuted.

We Must Never Give In, Never Give Up

Never give in – never, never, never, never, in nothing great or small, large or petty, never give in except to convictions of honor and good sense. Never yield to force; never yield to the apparently overwhelming might of the enemy.

~ Winston Churchill

B. BREAK IT DOWN! Every soldier's commitment will be tested and tested again. We simply must work the plan, make the sacrifice, and not give in – one day at a time!

1. *Don't grow weary,* Rev. 2.2-3 – I know your works, your toil and your patient endurance, and how you cannot bear with those who are evil, but have tested those who call themselves apostles and are not, and found them to be false. [3] I know you are enduring patiently and bearing up for my name's sake, and you have not grown weary.

2. *Don't give up,* Gal. 6.7-10 – Do not be deceived: God is not mocked, for whatever one sows, that will he also reap. [8] For the one who sows to his own flesh will from the flesh reap corruption, but the one who sows to the Spirit will from the Spirit reap eternal life. [9] And let us not grow weary of doing good, for in due season we will reap, if we do not give up. [10] So then, as we have opportunity, let us do good to everyone, and especially to those who are of the household of faith.

3. *Don't shrink back,* Heb. 10.35-39 – Therefore do not throw away your confidence, which has a great reward. [36] For you have need of endurance, so that when you have done the will of God you may receive what is promised. [37] For, "Yet a little while, and the coming one will come and will not delay; [38] but my righteous one shall live by faith, and if he shrinks back, my soul has no pleasure in him." [39] But we are not of those who shrink back and are destroyed, but of those who have faith and preserve their souls.

C. CHECK THIS OUT. The apostles exhorted believers to hang tough, even in the face of trial and resistance.

1. *They were exhorted to remain faithful to the Lord with steadfast purpose,* Acts 11.20-23 – But there were some of them, men of Cyprus and Cyrene, who on coming to Antioch spoke to the Hellenists also, preaching the Lord Jesus. [21] And the hand of the Lord was with them, and a great number who believed turned to the Lord. [22] The report of this came to the ears of the church in Jerusalem, and they sent Barnabas to Antioch. [23] When he came and saw the grace of God, he was glad, and he exhorted them all to remain faithful to the Lord with steadfast purpose.

> # There Are
> # NO Shortcuts
> To
> # Any Place
> # Worth Going

2. *They were told that they would enter the Kingdom only after enduring persecution,* Acts 14.21-23 – When they had preached the gospel to that city and had made many disciples, they returned to Lystra and to Iconium and to Antioch, [22] strengthening the souls of the disciples, encouraging them to continue in the faith, and saying that through many tribulations we must enter the kingdom of God. [23] And when they had appointed elders for them in every church, with prayer and fasting they committed them to the Lord in whom they had believed.

3. *They were told that they could not endure alone: they were to stand together or not at all!,* Phil. 1.27-28 – Only let your manner of life be worthy of the gospel of Christ, so that whether I come and see you or am absent, I may hear of you that you are standing firm in one spirit, with one mind striving side by side for the faith of the gospel, [28] and not frightened in anything by your opponents. This is a clear sign to them of their destruction, but of your salvation, and that from God.

III. Connection: Learn to Wait – Overcome Frustration and Discouragement in Prayer. Learn to Stand Your Ground.

A. THE KEY PRINCIPLE. Discouragement breeds defeat, but prayer produces perseverance.

B. DISCOURAGEMENT BREEDS DEFEAT. Discouragement feeds on the idea that things won't change, get any better, or will ever be overcome. Be careful of doubt, for it fuels discouragement!

1. *No matter what, remember God's got a hold on you!,* Ps. 37.23-24 – The steps of a man are established by the LORD, when he delights in his way; [24] though he fall, he shall not be cast headlong, for the LORD upholds his hand.

2. *God has established us, anointed us, and sealed us – in order that we can go on!,* 2 Cor. 1.21-22 – And it is God who establishes us with you in Christ, and has anointed us, [22] and who has also put his seal on us and given us his Spirit in our hearts as a guarantee.

3. *God uses trial and trouble to build us into qualified spiritual warriors!*

To Gain the Reward, God's Warrior Must Persevere in the Midst of Trial

Patience is an active endurance of opposition, not a passive resignation. Patience and patient are used to translate several Hebrew and Greek words. Patience is endurance, steadfastness, long suffering, and forbearance.

God is patient (Rom. 15:5). He is slow to anger in relation to the Hebrews (Exod. 34:6; Num. 14:18; Neh. 9:17; Ps. 86:15; Isa. 48:9; Hos. 11:8-9). The Hebrews were frequently rebellious, but God patiently dealt with them. Jesus' parable of the tenants depicted God's patience with his people (Mark 12:1-11). God's patience with sinners allows time for them to repent (Rom. 2:4), especially in the apparent delay of the return of Christ (2 Pet. 3:9-10).

God's people are to be patient. The psalmist learned to be patient when confronted with the prosperity of the wicked (Ps. 37:1-3, 9-13, 34-38). Christians should face adversity patiently (Rom. 5:3-5). Patience is a fruit of the Spirit (Gal. 5:22). Christian love is patient (1 Cor. 13:4,7). Ministers are to be patient (2 Cor. 6:6).

Christians need patient endurance in the face of persecution. Hebrews stressed endurance as the alternative to shrinking back during adversity (Heb. 6:9-15; 10:32-39). Jesus is the great example of endurance (Heb. 12:1-3). Perseverance is part of maturity (James 1:2-4). Job's perseverance is another example for suffering Christians (James 5:11). John frequently highlighted the patient endurance of Christians (Rev. 2:2,19; 3:10; 13:10; 14:12). Christian patience is ultimately a gift from God (Rom. 15:5-6; 2 Thess. 3:5).

~ Warren Williams. "Patience" in *Holman Bible Dictionary*, elec. ed. 2012.

a. *It produces proven character,* Rom. 5.3-4 – Not only that, but we rejoice in our sufferings, knowing that suffering produces endurance, [4] and endurance produces character, and character produces hope.

b. *It produces steadfastness,* James 1.3-4 – for you know that the testing of your faith produces steadfastness. [4] And let steadfastness have its full effect, that you may be perfect and complete, lacking in nothing.

SESSION 3: LEARN TO WAIT • 57

C. **PRAYER PRODUCES PERSEVERANCE.** All human beings everywhere are engaged in a massive battle for the universe, whether they are aware of it or not, Gen. 3.15.

The Holy Spirit: God's Power to Persevere in Trial

Empowerment for spiritual battle comes only from the Holy Spirit. He alone can equip and empower believers to endure in the face of protracted, difficult, and harsh battles, through his indwelling strength.

* He provides power to live and to grow, cf. Isa. 11.2-3; see also Isa. 42.1.
* The Spirit **enables God's warriors to serve** with honor, Ezek. 36.26-27; see also Jer. 31.33.
* The Holy Spirit supplies God's people with **prophecy and visions** Joel 2.28-29; cf. Acts 2.17-18.
* The Holy Spirit is revealed through biblical images: his power: **oil**, 1 Sam. 10.1; 16.13; the **arm of God**, Isa. 63.11-12; the **hand of God**, Ezek. 3.14; 37.1; the **breath of God**, Ezek. 37.
* He is God, his works revealed in **creation**, Gen. 1.2; Job 33.4; Ps. 104.30; in acts of **battle and war**, Judg. 14.19; 3.10; 6.34; 11.29; 14.6; 15.14; 1 Sam. 11.6; 16.13; and in the **lives of his servants**, Mic. 3.8; See also Num. 11.17; 1 Sam. 10.6, 10.
* Jesus was filled with the Spirit's power, demonstrated at his conception and birth, Luke 1.35; his teaching and ministry; Matt. 7.28-29; 12.28; Mark 1.22, 27; Luke 4.14; 5.17; Acts 10.38; in his resurrection, Rom. 1.4; 8.11; 1 Tim. 3.16; 1 Pet. 3.18

The Holy Spirit empowered the apostles and early Christians, who endured much trial and suffering. His powerful presence enabled them to fulfil the church's mission in their lifetime, especially in their witness and preaching, Acts 1.8 with Luke 24.49; Acts 6.10; 16.7; 1 Cor. 2.4; 1 Thess. 1.5.

---

1. *Consistent, fervent prayer enables you not to faint or give up,* Luke 18.1-8 – And he told them a parable to the effect that they ought always to pray and not lose heart. [2] He said, "In a certain city there was a judge who neither feared God nor respected man. [3] And there was a widow in that city who kept coming to him and saying, 'Give me justice against my adversary.' [4] For a while he refused, but afterward he said

to himself, 'Though I neither fear God nor respect man, [5] yet because this widow keeps bothering me, I will give her justice, so that she will not beat me down by her continual coming.'" [6] And the Lord said, "Hear what the unrighteous judge says. [7] And will not God give justice to his elect, who cry to him day and night? Will he delay long over them? [8] I tell you, he will give justice to them speedily. Nevertheless, when the Son of Man comes, will he find faith on earth?"

"If we pull this off, we'll eat like kings."

2. *Pray at all times for it keeps you alert and helps you to endure,* Eph. 6.14-18 – Stand therefore, having fastened on the belt of truth, and having put on the breastplate of righteousness, [15] and, as shoes for your feet, having put on the readiness given by the gospel of peace. [16] In all circumstances take up the shield of faith, with which you can extinguish all the flaming darts of the evil one; [17] and take the helmet of salvation, and the sword of the Spirit, which is the word of God, [18] praying at all times in the Spirit, with all prayer and supplication. To that end keep alert with all perseverance, making supplication for all the saints.

1 Cor. 15.58 – Therefore, my beloved brothers, be steadfast, immovable, always abounding in the work of the Lord, knowing that in the Lord your labor is not in vain.

As unwavering warriors of Christ's unshakeable Kingdom, we must learn to . . .

- *Work the Plan:* Learn the discipline of following strategy
- *Make the Sacrifice:* Unconditionally surrender all to represent Christ
- LEARN TO WAIT: *Endure trial and struggle as you seek God's leading and will*

SIAFU

UNSHAKEABLE KINGDOM

PLAN · SACRIFICE · WAIT

HONOR

UNWAVERING WARRIOR

REPRESENT

Appendix

APPENDIX 1
The Story of God: Our Sacred Roots

Rev. Dr. Don L. Davis

The LORD God is the source, sustainer, and end of all things in the heavens and earth. All things were formed and exist by his will and for his eternal glory, the triune God, Father, Son, and Holy Spirit, Rom. 11.36.

	THE TRIUNE GOD'S UNFOLDING DRAMA *God's Self-Revelation in Creation, Israel, and Christ*			THE CHURCH'S PARTICIPATION IN GOD'S UNFOLDING DRAMA *Fidelity to the Apostolic Witness to Christ and His Kingdom*			
	The Objective Foundation: The Sovereign Love of God *God's Narration of His Saving Work in Christ*			The Subjective Practice: Salvation by Grace through Faith *The Redeemed's Joyous Response to God's Saving Work in Christ*			
The Alpha and the Omega	**Christus Victor**	**Come, Holy Spirit**	**Your Word Is Truth**	**The Great Confession**	**His Life in Us**	**Living in the Way**	**Reborn to Serve**
The Author of the Story	*The Champion of the Story*	*The Interpreter of the Story*	*The Testimony of the Story*	*The People of the Story*	*Re-enactment of the Story*	*Embodiment of the Story*	*Continuation of the Story*
The Father as Director	Jesus as Lead Actor	The Spirit as Narrator	Scripture as Script	As Saints, Confessors	As Worshipers, Ministers	As Followers, Sojourners	As Servants, Ambassadors
Christian Worldview	Communal Identity	Spiritual Experience	Biblical Authority	Orthodox Theology	Priestly Worship	Congregational Discipleship	Kingdom Witness
Theistic and Trinitarian Vision	Christ-centered Foundation	Spirit-Indwelt and -Filled Community	Canonical and Apostolic Witness	Ancient Creedal Affirmation of Faith	Weekly Gathering in Christian Assembly	Corporate, Ongoing Spiritual Formation	Active Agents of the Reign of God
Sovereign Willing	Messianic Representing	Divine Comforting	Inspired Testifying	Truthful Retelling	Joyful Excelling	Faithful Indwelling	Hopeful Compelling
Creator True Maker of the Cosmos	Recapitulation Typos and Fulfillment of the Covenant	Life-Giver Regeneration and Adoption	Divine Inspiration God-breathed Word	The Confession of Faith Union with Christ	Song and Celebration Historical Recitation	Pastoral Oversight Shepherding the Flock	Explicit Unity Love for the Saints
Owner Sovereign Disposer of Creation	Revealer Incarnation of the Word	Teacher Illuminator of the Truth	Sacred History Historical Record	Baptism into Christ Communion of Saints	Homilies and Teachings Prophetic Proclamation	Shared Spirituality Common Journey through the Spiritual Disciplines	Radical Hospitality Evidence of God's Kingdom Reign
Ruler Blessed Controller of All Things	Redeemer Reconciler of All Things	Helper Endowment and the Power	Biblical Theology Divine Commentary	The Rule of Faith Apostles' Creed and Nicene Creed	The Lord's Supper Dramatic Re-enactment	Embodiment Anamnesis and Prolepsis through the Church Year	Extravagant Generosity Good Works
Covenant Keeper Faithful Promisor	Restorer Christ, the Victor over the powers of evil	Guide Divine Presence and Shekinah	Spiritual Food Sustenance for the Journey	The Vincentian Canon Ubiquity, antiquity, universality	Eschatological Foreshadowing The Already/Not Yet	Effective Discipling Spiritual Formation in the Believing Assembly	Evangelical Witness Making Disciples of All People Groups

APPENDIX 2

From Before to Beyond Time: The Plan of God and Human History

Adapted from Suzanne de Dietrich. *God's Unfolding Purpose*. Philadelphia: Westminster Press, 1976.

I. Before Time (Eternity Past) 1 Cor. 2.7
   A. The Eternal Triune God
   B. God's Eternal Purpose
   C. The Mystery of Iniquity
   D. The Principalities and Powers

II. Beginning of Time (Creation and Fall) Gen. 1.1
   A. Creative Word
   B. Humanity
   C. Fall
   D. Reign of Death and First Signs of Grace

III. Unfolding of Time (God's Plan Revealed through Israel) Gal. 3.8
   A. Promise (Patriarchs)
   B. Exodus and Covenant at Sinai
   C. Promised Land
   D. The City, the Temple, and the Throne (Prophet, Priest, and King)
   E. Exile
   F. Remnant

IV. Fullness of Time (Incarnation of the Messiah) Gal. 4.4-5
   A. The King Comes to His Kingdom
   B. The Present Reality of His Reign
   C. The Secret of the Kingdom: the Already and the Not Yet
   D. The Crucified King
   E. The Risen Lord

V. The Last Times (The Descent of the Holy Spirit) Acts 2.16-18
   A. Between the Times: the Church as Foretaste of the Kingdom
   B. The Church as Agent of the Kingdom
   C. The Conflict Between the Kingdoms of Darkness and Light

VI. The Fulfillment of Time (The Second Coming) Matt. 13.40-43
   A. The Return of Christ
   B. Judgment
   C. The Consummation of His Kingdom

VII. Beyond Time (Eternity Future) 1 Cor. 15.24-28
   A. Kingdom Handed Over to God the Father
   B. God as All in All

From Before to Beyond Time
Scriptures for Major Outlines Points

I. Before Time (Eternity Past)
1 Cor. 2.7 (ESV) - But we impart a secret and hidden wisdom of God, which God decreed before the ages for our glory (cf. Titus 1.2).

II. Beginning of Time (Creation and Fall)
Gen. 1.1 (ESV) - In the beginning, God created the heavens and the earth.

III. Unfolding of Time (God's Plan Revealed Through Israel)
Gal. 3.8 (ESV) - And the Scripture, foreseeing that God would justify the Gentiles by faith, preached the Gospel beforehand to Abraham, saying, "In you shall all the nations be blessed" (cf. Rom. 9.4-5).

IV. Fullness of Time (The Incarnation of the Messiah)
Gal. 4.4-5 (ESV) - But when the fullness of time had come, God sent forth his Son, born of woman, born under the law, to redeem those who were under the law, so that we might receive adoption as sons.

V. The Last Times (The Descent of the Holy Spirit)
Acts 2.16-18 (ESV) - But this is what was uttered through the prophet Joel: "'And in the last days it shall be,' God declares, 'that I will pour out my Spirit on all flesh, and your sons and your daughters shall prophesy, and your young men shall see visions, and your old men shall dream dreams; even on my male servants and female servants in those days I will pour out my Spirit, and they shall prophesy.'"

VI. The Fulfillment of Time (The Second Coming)
Matt. 13.40-43 (ESV) - Just as the weeds are gathered and burned with fire, so will it be at the close of the age. The Son of Man will send his angels, and they will gather out of his Kingdom all causes of sin and all lawbreakers, and throw them into the fiery furnace. In that place there will be weeping and gnashing of teeth. Then the righteous will shine like the sun in the Kingdom of their Father. He who has ears, let him hear.

VII. Beyond Time (Eternity Future)
1 Cor. 15.24-28 (ESV) - Then comes the end, when he delivers the Kingdom to God the Father after destroying every rule and every authority and power. For he must reign until he has put all his enemies under his feet. The last enemy to be destroyed is death. For "God has put all things in subjection under his feet." But when it says, "all things are put in subjection," it is plain that he is excepted who put all things in subjection under him. When all things are subjected to him, then the Son himself will also be subjected to him who put all things in subjection under him, that God may be all in all.

APPENDIX 3

Jesus of Nazareth: The Presence of the Future

Rev. Dr. Don L. Davis

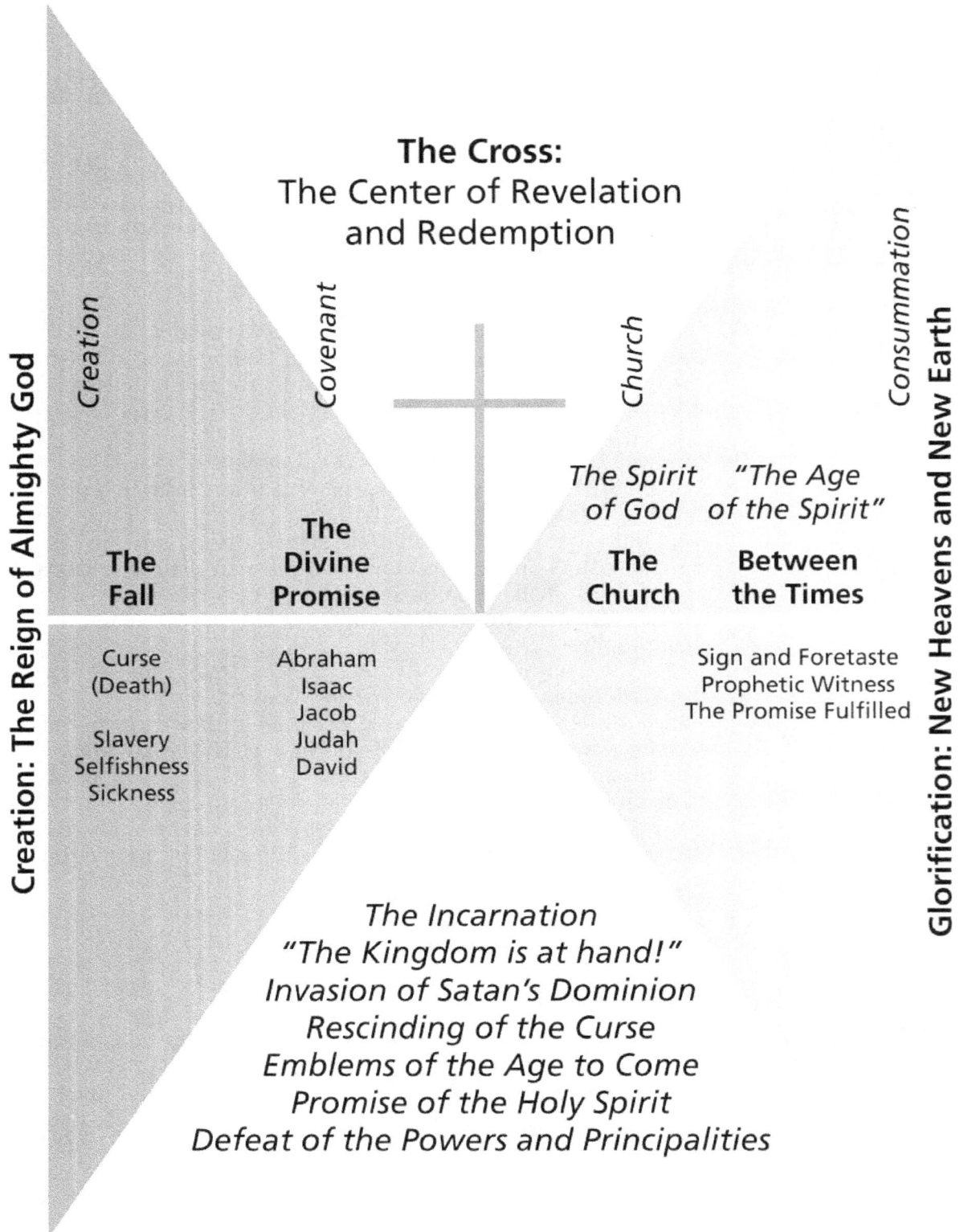

The Cross:
The Center of Revelation
and Redemption

Creation

Covenant

Church

Consummation

Creation: The Reign of Almighty God

Glorification: New Heavens and New Earth

The Spirit   "The Age
of God   of the Spirit"

**The
Divine
Promise**

**The
Fall**

**The   Between
Church   the Times**

Curse   Abraham
(Death)   Isaac
            Jacob
Slavery   Judah
Selfishness   David
Sickness

Sign and Foretaste
Prophetic Witness
The Promise Fulfilled

The Incarnation
"The Kingdom is at hand!"
Invasion of Satan's Dominion
Rescinding of the Curse
Emblems of the Age to Come
Promise of the Holy Spirit
Defeat of the Powers and Principalities

APPENDIX 4

Fit to Represent: Multiplying Disciples of the Kingdom of God

Rev. Dr. Don L. Davis

Luke 10.16 (ESV) - The one who hears you hears me, and the one who rejects you rejects me, and the one who rejects me rejects him who sent me.

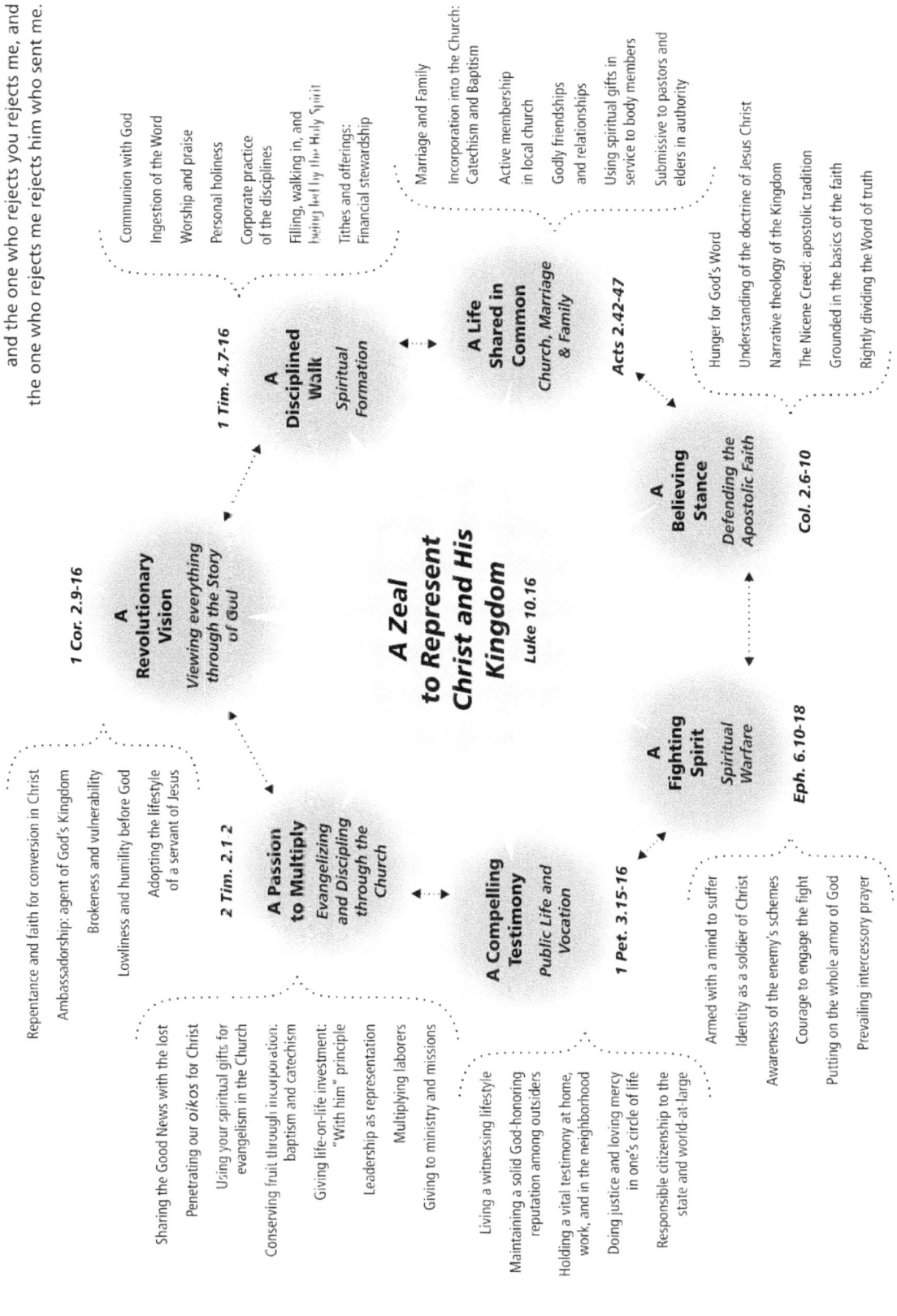

A Zeal to Represent Christ and His Kingdom
Luke 10.16

A Revolutionary Vision
Viewing everything through the Story of God
1 Cor. 2.9-16

- Repentance and faith for conversion in Christ
- Ambassadorship: agent of God's Kingdom
- Brokeness and vulnerability
- Lowliness and humility before God
- Adopting the lifestyle of a servant of Jesus

A Disciplined Walk
Spiritual Formation
1 Tim. 4.7-16

- Communion with God
- Ingestion of the Word
- Worship and praise
- Personal holiness
- Corporate practice of the disciplines
- Filling, walking in, and being led by the Holy Spirit
- Tithes and offerings: Financial stewardship

A Life Shared in Common
Church, Marriage & Family
Acts 2.42-47

- Marriage and Family
- Incorporation into the Church: Catechism and Baptism
- Active membership in local church
- Godly friendships and relationships
- Using spiritual gifts in service to body members
- Submissive to pastors and elders in authority

A Believing Stance
Defending the Apostolic Faith
Col. 2.6-10

- Hunger for God's Word
- Understanding of the doctrine of Jesus Christ
- Narrative theology of the Kingdom
- The Nicene Creed: apostolic tradition
- Grounded in the basics of the faith
- Rightly dividing the Word of truth

A Passion to Multiply
Evangelizing and Discipling through the Church
2 Tim. 2.1-2

- Sharing the Good News with the lost
- Penetrating our *oikos* for Christ
- Using your spiritual gifts for evangelism in the Church
- Conserving fruit through incorporation: baptism and catechism
- Giving life-on-life investment: "With him" principle
- Leadership as representation
- Multiplying laborers
- Giving to ministry and missions

A Compelling Testimony
Public Life and Vocation
1 Pet. 3.15-16

- Living a witnessing lifestyle
- Maintaining a solid God-honoring reputation among outsiders
- Holding a vital testimony at home, work, and in the neighborhood
- Doing justice and loving mercy in one's circle of life
- Responsible citizenship to the state and world-at-large

A Fighting Spirit
Spiritual Warfare
Eph. 6.10-18

- Armed with a mind to suffer
- Identity as a soldier of Christ
- Awareness of the enemy's schemes
- Courage to engage the fight
- Putting on the whole armor of God
- Prevailing intercessory prayer

APPENDIX 5

The Hump

Rev. Dr. Don L. Davis • 1 Timothy 4.9-16; Hebrews 5.11-14

The Baby Christian
The New Believer and the Spiritual Disciplines

Awkwardness

Unskillfulness

Mistakes

Roughness

Sporadic Behavior

Uncomfortableness

Inefficiency

Novice-Level Performance

Heart Desire
A Clear Goal
Feasible Plan
Solid Support
Correct Knowledge
Faithful Effort
Good Examples
Extended Period of Time
Longsuffering

Regular, correct application of the spiritual disciplines

The Mature Christian
The Mature Believer and the Spiritual Disciplines

Faithful Application

Gracefulness

Automatic response

Comfortableness

Personal Satisfaction

Excellence

Expertise

Training Others

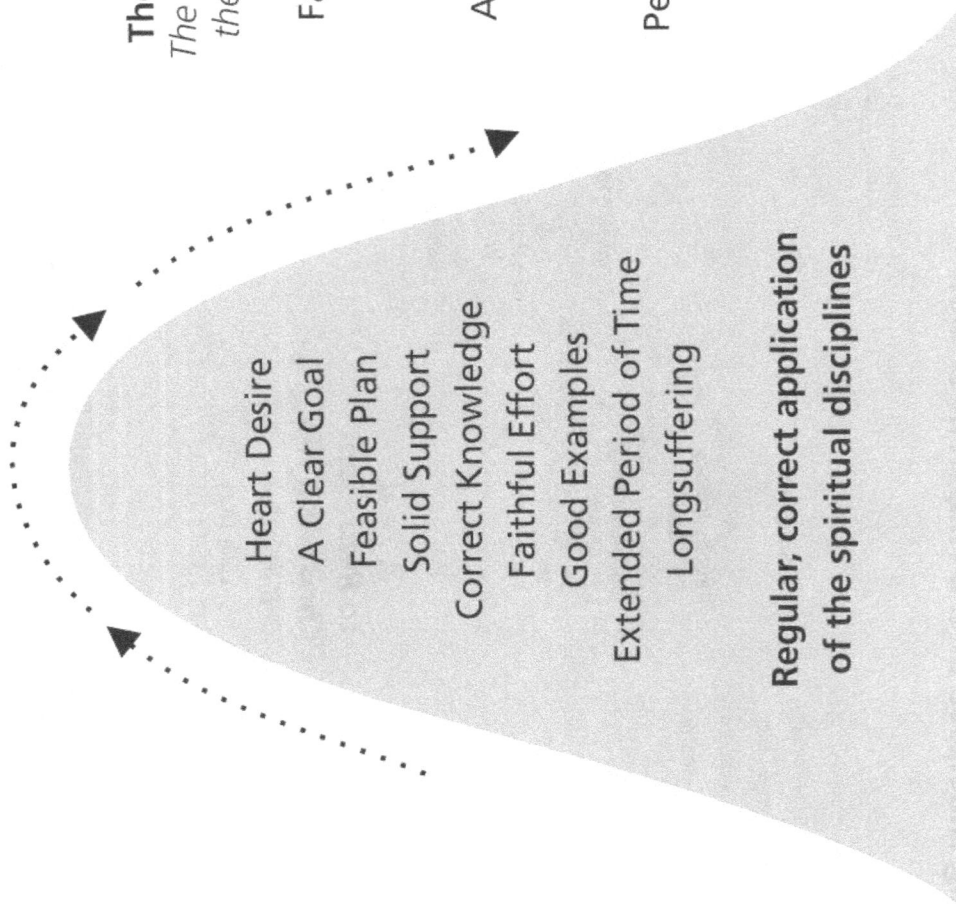

Steps to Equipping Others
Rev. Dr. Don L. Davis

Step One
You become a Master at it, striving toward mastery by practicing it with regularity, excellence, and enjoyment. You must learn to do it, and do it excellently. While you need not be perfect, you should be able to do it, be doing it regularly, and growing in your practice of it. This is the most fundamental principle of all mentoring and discipling. You cannot teach what you do not know or cannot do, and when your Apprentice is fully trained, they will become like you (Luke 6.40).

Step Two
You select an Apprentice who also desires to develop mastery of the thing, one who is teachable, faithful, and available. Jesus called the Twelve to be with him, and to send them out to preach (Mark 3.14). His relationship was clear, neither vague nor coerced. The roles and responsibilities of the relationship must be carefully outlined, clearly discussed, and openly agreed upon.

Step Three
You instruct and model the task **in the presence of and accompanied by** *your Apprentice.* He/she comes alongside you to listen, observe, and watch. You do it with regularity and excellence, and your Apprentice comes along "for the ride." who is brought along to see how it is done. A picture is worth a thousand words. This sort of non-pressure participant observation is critical to in-depth training (2 Tim. 2.2; Phil. 4.9).

Step Four
You do the task and **practice the thing together.** Having modeled the act for your Apprentice in many ways and at many times, you now invite them to cooperate with you by becoming a partner-in-training, working together on the task. The goal is to do the task together, taking mutual responsibility. You coordinate your efforts, working together in harmony to accomplish the thing.

Step Five
Your Apprentice does the task on their own, **in the presence of and accompanied by you.** You provide opportunity to your Apprentice to practice the thing in your presence while you watch and listen. You make yourself available to help, but offer it in the background; you provide counsel, input, and guidance as they request it, but they do the

task. Afterwards, you evaluate and clarify anything you may have observed as you accompanied your Apprentice (2 Cor. 11.1).

Step Six

Your Apprentice does the thing solo, practicing it regularly, automatically, and excellently **until mastery of the thing is gained**. After your Apprentice has done the task under your supervision excellently, he/she is ready to be released to make the thing his/her own by habituating the act in his/her own life. You are a co-doer with your Apprentice; both of you are doing the task without coercion or aid from the other. The goal is familiarity and skillfulness in the task (Heb. 5.11-15).

Step Seven

Your Apprentice **becomes a Mentor of others**, *selecting other faithful Apprentices to equip and train*. The training process bears fruit when the Apprentice, having mastered the thing you have equipped him/her to do, becomes a trainer of others. This is the heart of the discipling and training process (Heb. 5.11-14; 2 Tim. 2.2).

APPENDIX 7

Laws of Sowing and Reaping

Rev. Dr. Don L. Davis

| The Laws of Sowing and Reaping: Personal Discipline and Fruitfulness ||
The Law	The Explanation
You will reap what you sow	Sow to the Spirit and reap God's best
You will reap what others have sown	Transcend the harvest you have inherited
You reap the same in kind as what you sow	Choose wisely what you want to reap before you sow
You reap in proportion to what you sow	Sow more to get more in return
You reap in a different season than when you sow	Learn to be patient as you await the harvest
You reap more than what you sow	It is going to be better (or worse) than you gave
You can always transcend last year's harvest	God gives the growth, so trust in him alone

We cannot help but see that the [people] who have achieved wonders in modern science and technology are [people] of very great inner discipline. No one has succeeded by following the path of least resistance.

~ Elton Trueblood. *The Yoke of Christ.*
Waco, TX: Word Books, 1958. p. 128.

Prayer and Affirmation to God

Do not be deceived: God is not mocked, for whatever one sows, that will he also reap. [8] For the one who sows to his own flesh will from the flesh reap corruption, but the one who sows to the Spirit will from the Spirit reap eternal life. [9] And let us not grow weary of doing good, for in due season we will reap, if we do not give up.

~ Galatians 6.7-9

APPENDIX 8

From Deep Ignorance to Credible Witness

Rev. Dr. Don L. Davis

Witness - Ability to give witness and teach
2 Tim. 2.2
Matt. 28.18-20
1 John 1.1-4
Prov. 20.6
2 Cor. 5.18-21

And the things you have heard me say in the presence of many witnesses entrust to reliable men who will also be qualified to teach others.
~ 2 Tim. 2.2

8

Lifestyle - Consistent appropriation and habitual practice based on beliefs
Heb. 5.11-6.2
Eph. 4.11-16
2 Pet. 3.18
1 Tim. 4.7-10

And Jesus increased in wisdom and in stature, and in favor with God and man.
~ Luke 2.52

7

Demonstration - Expressing conviction in corresponding conduct, speech, and behavior
James 2.14-26
2 Cor. 4.13
2 Pet. 1.5-9
1 Thess. 1.3-10

Nevertheless, at your word I will let down the net.
~ Luke 5.5

6

Conviction - Committing oneself to think, speak, and act in light of information
Heb. 2.3-4
Heb. 11.1, 6
Heb. 3.15-19
Heb. 4.2-6

Do you believe this?
~ John 11.26

5

Discernment - Understanding the meaning and implications of information
John 16.13
Eph. 1.15-18
Col. 1.9-10
Isa. 6.10; 29.10

Do you understand what you are reading?
~ Acts 8.30

4

Knowledge - Ability to recall and recite information
2 Tim. 3.16-17
1 Cor. 2.9-16
1 John 2.20-27
John 14.26

For what does the Scripture say?
~ Rom. 4.3

3

Interest - Responding to ideas or information with both curiosity and openness
Ps. 42.1-2
Acts 9.4-5
John 12.21
1 Sam. 3.4-10

We will hear you again on this matter.
~ Acts 17.32

2

Awareness - General exposure to ideas and information
Mark 7.6-8
Acts 19.1-7
John 5.39-40
Matt. 7.21-23

At that time, Herod the tetrarch heard about the fame of Jesus.
~ Matt. 14.1

1

Ignorance - Unfamiliarity with information due to naivete, indifference, or hardness
Eph. 4.17-19
Ps. 2.1-3
Rom. 1.21; 2.19
1 John 2.11

Who is the Lord that I should heed his voice?
~ Exod. 5.2

0